DESERT

Desert
© Eric Larsh / Cathexis Northwest Press

No part of this book may be reproduced without written permission
of the publisher or author, except in reviews and articles.

First Printing: 2024

ISBN: 978-1-952869-90-7

Cover photo by Josh Sanabria
Designed and edited by C. M. Tollefson

Cathexis Northwest Press
cathexisnorthwestpress.com

DESERT

**by
Eric Larsh**

Cathexis Northwest Press

Difficult to know what one means
—to be serious and to know what one means
George Oppen, Ballad

thin line of risen demarcation
guttering
ambient particles
expresses in evening shortwave filters

dragging pink the meridian flashes
flames ghosting out & between
browbeating of the hour's jealousy
& my hanging head
holy [UNEXPRESSED]–

–it makes roughly a motioning for support
waving soundlessly above it allowing for the ceaseless chain

– *vote*

 −it makes roughly
heavy black
dab

parabolic   primum mobile

& when all else fails

vote again

slabbed injunction bodies premia

you can't move
in this world yet
you can't horizon−

with some regularity
dependency
courtesy

I see it wrestling
the word with
it/self

doesn't it? –

folds into it
rouses it completely
         with the dust & duty anyway

doesn't it? –

little quantitative evidence
regarding collection
& deliberate maiming
& killing by humans
has been obtained

dirt
rock
sand
smoke
ash
bacteria
skin
hair

if we were to take this chance–

hold vigil

in a moonlit canyon
wrapped in our rags
using friction
naked heat to keep

our bodies warm
without disturbing
skittish deer mouse
tired creosote bush

–we predict

& on impact we hear it

what's left

paved / unpaved roads
& non-native invasive plant-life
& the threat of wildfire
& human populations
& prospective energy production
& habitat loss
& population fragmentation
& nutritional compromise
& soil erosion
& indirect impacts associated with increased human presence
–   illegal dumping / human subsidies for predators /
introduction of toxins

now that I think about it

—where are the butterflies

"I would never tell anyone that I found one here. It will hurt the homeowners' property values." –

I've been told that
time & again

sometimes it is

the removal of the thing

another piece-
meal ephemera
baked long in the heat

is it
comeuppance –
the indecipherable
message   caught; liminal
on a cross wind

summer smoke
a long-
patient body warm
to the idea;   spectering
glimpses phase
wild &
reluctant
–that image
a raised hand
at my eye
blocks a beaming   &
illiberal sun

poking my dried-blood beak   from this home I've stolen

evidence of breakfast
          this three color morning
          incriminatory

& if I leave again while the wind is acting
       the way it is
       I could be whipped
          from my senses
  – for now I'll nibble at my underwing tenderly
         scratch   at the pillowy webs
          the dry twigs

Bird lands not too far out of my reach & when the sun sets, I see the mass of itself pour over the canyon wall. I wash in it, the whisper of its flowing revealing
a secret to me about a tortoise seemingly asleep at my side, the space I had cleared for something to lay my head on filled now with its testudinal smoothness. I let it lie there–motionless, though it always appears that way with a distance–you know, the rate at which it moves, deceiving, relative stillness
                                                                                          –feint lifelessness.

I have–in my sitting up here–learned to see movement in the image of unstirring.

bulldozers typically scrape the vegetation & topsoil into berms to prepare the sites for greenhouses, & water is often stolen from agricultural wells / aqueducts / hydrants for irrigation

& this time it hadn't
counted the needles stuck in my knees – plucked
                    tanned for the ripe cliff face   what it was
                                        propagated –

said to eat the suncup leaves – understood
                    it's the early morning work   the sound of the gravel
                    scraping into a grid
                    ourselves evidenced only

                                                        in small footprints
                                        made from returning the rake

the rolling over

                    the most expressive
                    & clearest indication

                    dusk breaks
                            a domesticated

                    shade long
                                                over the willow tree
                            in the middle of
                    your backyard

I am under an obligation to say everything at once.

As habitat is degraded, lost, or fragmented

by anthropogenic barriers

inter-patch relationships may break down

resulting in a decreased

likelihood that recolonizations will occur

Acknowledge–
Move on–

tall cactus living outside
in the tortoise pen
sags under passing
heavy cover of clouds

clearly a
gesture of
desire
spired pinkish
& justified

– explosive

again the stuttering rain
in the fluting gutters

witness
to movement without agency

What are the critical linkages that need to be protected?

                                        exhausted image
                                surfaced & with the soft
                                surfaced weed blowed along
                                a carved brocade hung
                                at a rest stop–

How can we manage the remaining habitat matrix in ways that sustain ecological processes and habitat suitability for special status species?

                                        always been–don't
                                                ask

Fragmentation exacerbates negative trends by increasing the probability that isolated populations will suffer irreversible declines due to stochastic (unpredictable) effects acting on their smaller local abundances, especially when combined with multiple external threats within the population fragments.

no birds

rail spike
rusted over

sour red berries   color my tongue

for kisses sucked
my breath
from my body

dry grass   kindling
I save for a fire

series of earthquakes
in conversation

I ask as I did   make sense?

a dance around

the fissure

        looked deep in

For the states of the lower division
it's better to ask simply, *where
will it come from?* – it will come
from somewhere. Slow drip then

but those floods
have stopped coming. Safety,
cottonwood-willow barely in place
to shade the rosy boa, dreadful
heat in dead summer; *oh, no* –

a promise, something should be
done before it all dries up. Passing
again, talons dig
into the gentle gila, orange-
black manifest on the sandstone

do not coexist well with human development
& disturbances

                                      & essentially absent within
1km of areas with greater than 10% development

−urban development / cultivated agriculture / energy
development / surface mines & quarries / pipelines &
transmission lines / roads & railroads−

habitat affected by development is only likely to increase with
ongoing urban growth

Naked heads watch, wary
of powerlines. Some lost lives that way.

An afternoon snack
of stinking carrion.

Warning! Toxic!

–an economic boon?

here's to hoping it's roadkill;
died of natural causes

Cherubic

Carelessness

It has run through the soft matter. River, a porous genetic barrier through time. The recovery objective is to condition self-sustaining–*the population*–within each recovery unit into the future.
We have been gathered along the morphic beach, bathing in it.
I have been gathered by the thriving mirage.
Knowledge of the precise distribution is limited, & individual threats vary.

                          Absolute amount of habitat
                          lost.

The landscape, a revised broadsheet with the language barely legible in the creases, the leathered paper stiff, scarred from top to bottom, turned over through a labored hand. There is a beading eye to the valley's wanderers that live in it, lungs choked with silt.

                          I hesitate to say all that.

& the weakest way to describe

something
when all else fails

kaleidoscopic

brilliant word   means almost nothing

how dare it say –

definitionless
contrastless

meaning takes a microscope –

star-talking
duplicate

adrift –

people said

you were a big baby

walking earth

the story goes

tidal   hairy

ignite   transfer

I misheard it

as *bead* of tender-
ness

to turn it over
so it can walk on
with the belly of its shell

    a rare encounter

we come to find out
that to play in the dirt with them
the barrel colored same as the cedar tree

    it could hurt some, too

    a moth
lifting Joshuas up
across itself

glassy dune stretching miles

relinquishes–

& when all else fails
the language of & for

at its most inconsiderate–

slips behind a favorite
hiding place, ducked from view;

26

Didn't I ask you before? –

always in mind of that backyard
of the soul;

your words
not mine; I could never be

so mawkish, so trusting–

however
I am not an unborn cavern

gape in the mammoth landscape
unfolding–wholly overturned

us again at the saddle,
scraping the earth
through the gash of it–

exclusion fencing tied into culverts, underpasses or overpasses, or other passages below roads
in the habitat, would limit vehicular mortality

would provide opportunities; more movement across

buried in the sand
was something–

I dug up ages ago
    a dogged compulsion maybe
& I heard the thing whistle :

crushed under
small paws &
flesh-colored
cloud

for what it is worth

the fragment

hangs–on

is it music

21,000 men it took to build it,

—

ruins are easily visible
now that the water is low enough

reservoir
ghost town

I am–

atom after atom; working
                         emotional salt–*without question*
loose sand–
             & I believe in the page without question

at the canyon floor   pittered echoes remain heard;

the valley calling back   *without question*

Fresh water is rare, covering just 0.8% of the Earth's surface.

evokes
discussion
of benefit

necessitates
wildfire
as it could
be
or have been

when–

thunder
is the only sound

even when–
it comes

unprepared &
underutilized

when
what appears true

is dismissed

as hyperbole

–what's that

I found

I cannot argue with the lights

I cannot argue with the waters

I cannot argue with the measure

I cannot argue with the mode

I cannot argue with the strain

I cannot argue with the weeds

I cannot argue with the ground

Edge of the lake waves out as I drink from it, hands cupped and dripping; my feet turned outward–
knees bent deep. Sferic messages rupture dribbling silence,
speak once or twice; verse; line–I am
& am not participant. Not profound or even advice. The cave spits out whatever it was they looked for.

cane & shrub
surround me
gulp me down

saltcedar gathers in dense thickets   its root system
digs down   deep
accesses water unavailable to other plants

giant reed thrives in the riparian area
                alters the ecosystem
is nearly impossible to combat

familiar—in its own way

ask again

when

who am I to judge

seeing cracks
form
where I stand
unmoving

conscious
structure built
without permission;
groans

wither–
my hand
touched
to my ear

it sounds;
together;

swish

rattle

burble

squinch

Deep roots; momentary
satisfaction across the board –

They say it's barnacled cement
that has kept the real shame of it hidden,
trespass of the boats couldn't reveal it,
but it was never a secret as such.

is it all happening

on the surface

of a bubble

time and again?

I think

true

given

I heard it

from

a trusted

source

−what always runs but never
       walks often murmurs never
           talks has a bed never
              sleeps has a mouth but never
                        eats−

if time & resources are limited, prioritize maintenance based on current & forecasted distributions

of course
that is
most obvious
without question

−How many people died building it?

The official number of fatalities involved is 96. These were men who died at the site
(classified as "industrial fatalities")
from such causes as drowning, blasting, falling rocks or slides, falls from the canyon walls, being struck
by heavy equipment, truck accidents, etc.

Industrial fatalities do not include deaths from heat, pneumonia, heart trouble, etc.

−How many people are there, buried in the concrete?

The answer to that has−historically−been *none.*

mistaken

rain

for stardust;

for context

dust

Acknowledgments

Janelle Angelo, my partner in all things, thank you for your unconditional support and love.

My deepest gratitude and love to my parents and brother; without you, none of this would be possible.

To all of my friends that continue to believe in me, thank you.

Thank you to the Portland State University Creative Writing department and my instructors, John Beer and Consuelo Wise especially for your encouragement and feedback, without which *Desert* would not have been written. Thank you to the others at Portland State University that engaged with my work in some capacity: Michael Seidlinger, Leni Zumas, Janice Lee, Michele Glazer, Dan DeWeese, Hildy Miller, Elisabeth Ceppi, Thomas Fischer, and anyone else that should have been included here.

Thank you to Jay Butler, Joshua Stanek, Jessamyn Duckwall, Ambra Wilson, and Lora Kinkade. Your writing and critical eyes influenced this project greatly.

A heartfelt thanks to any writer or researcher that has contributed to my ever-evolving poetics. There are certainly too many to list.

Also Available
from
Cathexis Northwest Press:

Cathexis Northwest Press

Printed in the USA
CPSIA information can be obtained
at www.ICGtesting.com
LVHW061951130924
790798LV00011B/335